Fantastic Fairs

Street Fair

by Julie Murray

Dash!
LEVELED READERS
An Imprint of Abdo Zoom • abdobooks.com

3

3 Dash!
LEVELED READERS

Level 1 – Beginning
Short and simple sentences with familiar words or patterns for children who are beginning to understand how letters and sounds go together.

Level 2 – Emerging
Longer words and sentences with more complex language patterns for readers who are practicing common words and letter sounds.

Level 3 – Transitional
More developed language and vocabulary for readers who are becoming more independent.

THIS BOOK CONTAINS
RECYCLED MATERIALS

abdobooks.com

Published by Abdo Zoom, a division of ABDO, PO Box 398166, Minneapolis, Minnesota 55439. Copyright © 2020 by Abdo Consulting Group, Inc. International copyrights reserved in all countries. No part of this book may be reproduced in any form without written permission from the publisher. Dash!™ is a trademark and logo of Abdo Zoom.

Printed in the United States of America, North Mankato, Minnesota.
052019
092019

Photo Credits: iStock, Shutterstock
Production Contributors: Kenny Abdo, Jennie Forsberg, Grace Hansen, John Hansen
Design Contributors: Dorothy Toth, Neil Klinepier

Library of Congress Control Number: 2018963307

Publisher's Cataloging in Publication Data

Names: Murray, Julie, author.
Title: Street fair / by Julie Murray.
Description: Minneapolis, Minnesota : Abdo Zoom, 2020 | Series: Fantastic fairs |
    Includes online resources and index.
Identifiers: ISBN 9781532127267 (lib. bdg.) | ISBN 9781532128240 (ebook) |
    ISBN 9781532128738 (Read-to-me ebook)
Subjects: LCSH: Art fairs--Juvenile literature. | Handicraft festivals--Juvenile
    literature. | Fairs--Juvenile literature.
Classification: DDC 394.6--dc23

Table of Contents

Street Fair

A street fair is a gathering that takes place in a certain neighborhood or area. It is often held on the main streets of a community.

The streets are blocked off during a street fair. No cars are allowed. People can walk freely through the fair.

Many street fairs have a **theme**. There are art fairs, food fairs, and music fairs. About 30,000 people attend the Old Town Art Fair in Chicago, Illinois.

Street Fair History

Street fairs have been going on for many years. They started as a way to bring more business to a community. They had parades, food, and fireworks.

There was a lot of racial and political **tension** in the US in the 1970s. Then, street fairs were a way to help bring neighbors back together.

Today, street fairs are held all over the country. Some are small and are only a few blocks long. Others are huge and may spread over several city streets.

Well-Known Street Fairs

Mardi Gras is the largest street fair in the US. It is in New Orleans, Louisiana. More than 1.4 million people attend each year.

Sturgis Motorcycle Rally is a big street festival. Thousands of motorcycles pull into town for this 10-day affair. It is held in Sturgis, South Dakota.

Carnival in Rio de Janeiro, Brazil, is the largest street fair in the world. More than ten million people attend the five-day celebration each year. There is music, dancing, parades, and food.

More Facts

- The Carlsbad Village Faire claims to be the largest one-day street fair in the nation. More than 100,000 people fill the streets of Carlsbad, California.

- Jubilee Day in New York City is the largest one-day street fair on the east coast. More than 70,000 people enjoy food, games, entertainment, and carnival rides.

- South by Southwest (SXSW) is a 10-day festival that has turned into one big street fair. It is held in Austin, Texas, every March.

Glossary

Mardi Gras – a popular carnival celebration that takes place before the fasting season of Lent.

tension – mental or emotional strain.

theme – a particular setting or ambience to a venue or activity.

Index

Online Resources

Booklinks
NONFICTION NETWORK
FREE! ONLINE NONFICTION RESOURCES

To learn more about street fairs, please visit **abdobooklinks.com** or scan this QR code. These links are routinely monitored and updated to provide the most current information available.